Bo and Zop
learn how to be an
EARTHLING

HOW ARE EARTHLINGS THE SAME BUT DIFFERENT?

by Kirsty Holmes

🌳 **CRABTREE**
PUBLISHING COMPANY

Author: Kirsty Holmes

Editorial director: Kathy Middleton

Editors: Madeline Tyler, Janine Deschenes

Proofreader: Melissa Boyce

Graphic design: Dan Scas

**Production coordinator
 & Prepress technician:** Ken Wright

Print coordinator: Katherine Berti

Images

Shutterstock: Kravtzov p 13 bottom

All images are courtesy of Shutterstock.com, unless otherwise specified.

Alien Bo: delcarmat. Alien Zop: Roi and Roi. Background – PremiumArt. Vectors throughout: kearia.

Speech bubbles: Surrphoto.

All facts, statistics, web addresses and URLs in this book were verified as valid and accurate at time of writing. No responsibility for any changes to external websites or references can be accepted by either the author or publisher.

Library and Achives Canada Cataloguing in Publication

Title: How are earthlings the same but different? / Kirsty Holmes.
Other titles: Same but different
Names: Holmes, Kirsty, author.
Description: Series statement: Bo & Zop learn how to be an earthling |
   Originally published under title: Same but different: a book about diversity.
   King's Lynn: BookLife, 2020. | Includes index.
Identifiers: Canadiana (print) 20200225367 |
   Canadiana (ebook) 20200225375 |
   ISBN 9780778781172 (hardcover) |
   ISBN 9780778781219 (softcover) |
   ISBN 9781427125675 (HTML)
Subjects: LCSH: Cultural pluralism—Juvenile literature. | LCSH: Individual
   differences—Juvenile literature. | LCSH: Equality—Juvenile literature. |
   LCSH: Conduct of life—Juvenile literature.
Classification: LCC HM1271 .H65 2021 | DDC j305.8—dc23

Library of Congress Cataloging-in-Publication Data

Names: Holmes, Kirsty, author.
Title: How are earthlings the same but different? / Kirsty Holmes.
Description: New York : Crabtree Publishing Company, [2020] | Series: Bo &
   Zop learn how to be an earthling | Includes index.
Identifiers: LCCN 2020016273 (print) | LCCN 2020016274 (ebook) |
   ISBN 9780778781172 (hardcover) |
   ISBN 9780778781219 (paperback) |
   ISBN 9781427125675 (ebook)
Subjects: LCSH: Cultural pluralism--Juvenile literature. | Multiculturalism--
   Juvenile literature. | Individual differences--Juvenile literature.
Classification: LCC HM1271 .H646 2020 (print) | LCC HM1271 (ebook) |
   DDC 305.8--dc23
LC record available at https://lccn.loc.gov/2020016273
LC ebook record available at https://lccn.loc.gov/2020016274

Crabtree Publishing Company

www.crabtreebooks.com   1-800-387-7650

Published by Crabtree Publishing Company in 2021

©2020 BookLife Publishing Ltd

Printed in the U.S.A./072020/CG20200429

**Published in Canada
Crabtree Publishing**
616 Welland Avenue
St. Catharines, Ontario
L2M 5V6

**Published in the United States
Crabtree Publishing**
347 Fifth Ave
Suite 1402-145
New York, NY 10016

CONTENTS

Bo and Zop learn how to be an EARTHLING

Words with lines underneath, like this, can be found in the glossary on page 24.

SOMEWHERE IN THE SOLAR SYSTEM...

★

Look up into the night sky. How many stars do you see? One star shines the brightest. Maybe it is bigger than the others. Or maybe it is not a star at all. It could be a <u>satellite</u>. Or it could be...an alien spaceship!

★

Earth

Alien spaceship

Two brave aliens from planet Omegatron are on a mission to planet Earth. Their names are Bo and Zop. They want to learn all about Earthlings before they decide if Earth is safe to visit.

"I'm Bo. Can we go back home now?"

"I'm Zop! Can we be friends?"

Bo wants to learn what Earthlings are like. He sees a group of four Earthling friends. Each one is different. "Here are four types of Earthlings!" he thinks. "All Earthlings must fit into one of these four types." He starts to sort Earthlings into each group.

Earthling Groups

Group 1
Brown hair
Hazel eyes
Tall
Good at math

Group 2
Red hair
Blue eyes
Short
Likes to cook

Group 3
Black hair
Brown eyes
Medium height
Plays sports

Group 4
Blond hair
Green eyes
Very tall
Loves to draw

"This Earthling has blue eyes and brown hair. This one is short and plays sports. They do not fit into my groups!"

Soon, Bo has a problem. The fifth Earthling he sees does not fit into any of the four groups. Neither does the sixth, seventh, eighth, or ninth. Each Earthling is different from the last!

MANY DIFFERENCES

Bo has realized that Earthlings do not easily fit into groups. He has a lot to learn about them. From their hair and eye color to their skills and beliefs, no two Earthlings are the same!

"Instead of sorting them into groups, let's learn more about how Earthlings are different!"

"Zop, how will I learn about Earthlings if I can't sort them into groups?"

Bo knows that the fuzzy stuff on an Earthling's head is called hair. He sees straight and curly hair. He sees light hair and dark hair. He even sees hair with bright colors. Some Earthlings have a lot of hair and some have no hair at all!

"Earthlings also have many skin colors. But not a single one has green skin like me!"

Earthlings have different bodies too. Some Earthlings are tall. Others are short. Their body parts, such as ears, hands, and noses, are many shapes and sizes.

"These Earthlings look the same!"

"That's because they are identical twins, Bo."

Earthlings use their bodies to move. They move in many ways! They jump, wave, and dance. They also use their body parts to hear, talk, and see! Some Earthlings use special **devices** to help their bodies work well.

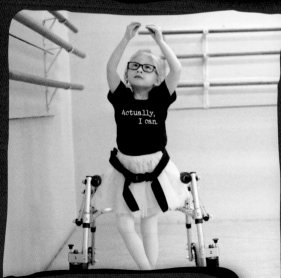

This girl uses a wheelchair to help her dance.

This boy uses a hearing aid to help him hear.

11

THE SAME BUT DIFFERENT

Bo is amazed. Even though Earthlings look different from each other, many things about them are the same too. They all need eyes to see and ears to hear. They all depend on their bodies to live, work, and play.

"Let's find out!"

"What other things are the same and different at the same time?"

This community depends on fishing for food and jobs.

Students in this school community learn about growing food.

These Earthlings are part of their religious community.

Together, Earthlings are part of one global community. They also belong to communities at home, school, and in their neighborhoods. There are many different kinds of communities.

"No two Earthling families are the same."

Every Earthling has a family. Some families have many members, and some have few. Families can even be made up of friends! Who is part of your family?

14

Many Earthlings follow a religion. They share beliefs with others. There are many kinds of religions!

Buddhist

"Many other Earthlings do not follow a religion. They still have beliefs, though!"

Christian

Muslim

Sikh

"I don't have a religion!"

Jewish

15

DIVERSITY IS IMPORTANT

It would be a very boring planet if every Earthling was exactly the same! Earthlings can learn new ideas and skills from each other. They can use their different skills to help each other succeed.

Have you ever learned something new from a friend? What is something you could teach others?

When Earthlings with different ideas, skills, and beliefs work together, they can solve problems and invent new things. Diversity is very important!

Engineers put their ideas together to solve problems.

These children put their skills together to make beautiful music.

ALL EQUAL

All Earthlings are part of a global community. It is important that every member of the community treats one another equally. This makes the global community a good place to live.

Being treated equally means that every Earthling has the same rights. They all deserve safety, respect, and freedom.

We are all Earthlings!

Even though every Earthling is different in their own special way, they should all share the same rights because they are all members of the global community.

GETTING ALONG

"Pizza is the best food. My family has the best recipe."

"No, tacos are the best. No one makes them better than my Grandma!"

"Look, Zop. These Earthlings aren't getting along very well."

"It is normal for Earthlings to disagree. They all have different ideas and opinions!"

An Earthling's ideas and opinions often come from their <u>background</u>. Earthlings have many different backgrounds, and many different ideas and opinions! It is important for them to remember that even though they might disagree, they should treat others with respect.

How do you show others you respect their ideas and opinions?

A WONDERFUL COMMUNITY

Bo and Zop have learned a lot about what makes Earthlings different and the same. They know that together, Earthlings make a wonderfully diverse global community.

How are you different from other Earthlings? How are you the same? Share your ideas with your friends. Ask them questions about their ideas too!

Bo has stopped trying to sort Earthlings into groups. Instead, he made a beautiful <u>collage</u> that shows how diverse they are.

"That is wonderful, Bo!"

"Earthlings are cool."

GLOSSARY

background — A person's experiences and knowledge

collage — A work of art with many pictures and materials glued to a surface

community — A group of people who live, work, and play in a place

devices — Equipment used for a special purpose

Earthlings — Human beings

engineers — People whose job it is to use math, science, and creative thinking to solve problems

global — Worldwide

opinions — Judgments based on personal experiences or knowledge

religious — Related to religion

respect — Viewing and treating someone or something with admiration and thoughtfulness

rights — Something, such as education, that humans should have or are entitled to

satellite — A human-made object that circles Earth or another space object

INDEX